SAPPHO'S MOON

Geoffrey Heptonstall

Acknowledgements

Some of these poems have been published in Ariadne's Thread, As It Ought to Be, The Bow Wow Shop, Caught in the Net, The Coffee House, The Drunken Llama, The English Chicago Review, Enigma, Incandescent, Ink Sweat & Tears, International Literary Quarterly, The Journal, Kalyna Review, The London Magazine, London Progressive Journal, Message in a Bottle, Nine Muses, Optimum, Pacific Review, Pangolin Review, The Patchwork Papers, The Pen, La Piccioletta Barca, Poesis, , Poetry Salzburg, Sarasvati, and The Write Place at the Write Time.

Venetian Whispers appeared in *Inspire*, a source book for Creative Writing, published by Goldsmith's College, University of London 2020

Voices was written for a masque, *Emperors for Tea*, devised by Clare Newton at the Savoy Hotel, London 2013

Ghost Walks was digitally broadcast as part of the Burning Man Festival, Nevada 2020

The Moor of Venice appeared in *Poetry in the Plague Year* anthology 2020

Of Calm First Light and *Another Memento* appeared in *Essential*, an Underground Writers anthology 2020

My particular thanks to Emma Brankin, Sasha Dugdale, Kate McLoughlin and Caryna Sharples. The greater debt is paid in these pages to my wife Debbie.

CONTENTS

A TABLE OF TRANSLATIONS 7

THE MAGICIAN'S SHADOW 9

CHANGING, VIEWING, PASSING 11

FORTUNE'S LODGING 12

THE FUTURE MAY SEEM WRITTEN 14

SAPPHO'S MOON 17

GENESIS 18

PYGMALION 19

BEGGAR'S BOUNTY 20

THE BACCHAE 21

THE MADNESS OF AJAX 22

ORPHEUS APPEARS 23

ACTAEON 24

ORPHEUS DESCENDING 25

POSEIDON: OF DESIRE 26

SYSYPHUS: OF PUNISHMENT 27

MINERVA: OF WISDOM 28

ANTIGONE: OF REVENGE 29

ODYSSEUS: OF WAR 30

ANOTHER HOMERIC MOMENT 31

THE FOUNDATION OF THE CITY OF WOMEN 32

ADVICE TO THE IMAGINATION 34

THE DREAM OF ADMIRAL ZHENG HE 35

VOICES 36

IN MEMORY OF LI YUI-SE 38

A LADY LAMENTED 39

A TREASURE OF THE WESTERN HAN DYNASTY 40

A DREAM OF XANADU 41

A DAY'S WORK FAR FROM THE CITY 43

REFLECTIONS ON A WINDOW IN LAN'TIEN 44

OF JADE AND IVORY 45
A WARRIOR RETURNS FROM BATTLE 47
SECONDS IN CHINA 48
OF CALM FIRST LIGHT, GROWING 50
PROLOGUE 52
A PLANTAGENET WEB 53
A MIDSUMMER NIGHT'S REVERIE 54
DANCING AT VERONA 55
SIR JOHN'S MIDNIGHT 56
A ROMAN HOLIDAY 57
MALVOLIO'S EPIPHANY 58
THE QUEEN OF EGYPT 59
THE MISTRESS OF CAWDOR 60
AMLETH 61
VENETIAN WHISPERS 62
THE STORM 64
THE MOOR OF VENICE 66
THE FOOL'S APOLOGY 67
THE POET'S HAND 68
CITY OF WORDS 70
THE HISTORY OF A CITY 73
BOSTON SQUARE 74
GHOST WALKS 75
BERLIN 78
A CROWN FOR THE QUEEN OF ELSEWHERE 79
SOUTH KENSINGTON 81
YORK 82
ELSEWHERE AT THE CITY'S BOUNDS 83
METRO 84
CODA 85
FIREBIRDS 86
MEMENTO 87
PROVIDENCE 89
JOHN BERRYMAN'S RECOVERY 91

A TABLE OF TRANSLATIONS

Reading from the original
to dare translate while speaking
as one word becomes another.
The objects before me are reflections
that lighten the shadows of meaning.
from the table I choose these things:

A leaf from a tree in the forest
where Cezanne worked in solitude.
Nature is seen as exacting art.
Like blossom in the wind,
like ice in the river thaw,
float the memories of St Victoire.

A shell from a strand on Inis Mór
is an intricate memorial
and a horn to summon inspiration
in a turning world.
These islands are a universe
encompassed by infinite ocean.

A butterfly paperweight in stone
impressed by a moment of beauty
that lingers in the mind so movingly.
It becomes the hum of wings
escaping the confines of chrysalis.
From the table I chose these things:

A polemic lies restlessly
eager for the insurgence
Ferlinghetti has promised
in words of stardust falling
as white water in the cataract.
His thoughts are timely metaphors.

The blade glides through the folds,
and an envelope reveals its secret.
I see the Silk Road in the ornate handle
my fingers hold almost in reverence
before the ceremony of opening
a letter sealed by her lips.

THE MAGICIAN'S SHADOW

What he touches turns to fire, then air,
then earth, then water.
Everything elemental,
acting out a primal scene.
His hand can gently
sift the dust encircling the world
of the mind at play.
The sound is the spring
that flows from harmony.

All that happens has been known
from the sun's first rising
on an awakening life.
There is a space where imagination enters,
only to fly into the shimmer of noon
where once was darkness
and never dare be again.

The romance is familiar:
a question in the fabric of time.
Threads of being are woven
of clouds and a clear sky.
Reality the riderless,
truth a critical simile
harnessed at once to the onlooker's eye.

A match for creation of a chrysalis
within the promise of late Lenten days.
All is waiting. And words, gathering wisdom,

consider the question of 'Why?'
'When?' is more certain.

For Peter Brook

CHANGING, VIEWING, PASSING

This much is known of art:
in the gallery a book of imaginings
reads the world as shape and colour.
It surely is the wisest counsel
that water is drawn from the well.
All else elaborates the earth-bound
fact of roots found somewhere down
Art has a life of shade and light,
seen to change at every viewing,
like landscapes in their seasons
where life resides at source.
All shall be found within
arabesques of experience,
original but human.
And there begins time passing.
That much is known, but not well.

FORTUNE'S LODGING

The shadow of his hand crossed the paper
when he moved the lamp for better light.
'God's image is in everything,',
he murmured, closing the book
when he could write no more.
Contraries crossed his mind.

He spat out the bite of fruit,
leaving a sour taste on his tongue.
For Lent he abstained from wine.
He took air in the garden.
Leaves of mint refreshed him,
but would not still the questions.

The night was not silent.
All the city passed his window.
His thinking was accustomed to sound.
The hammering of desks in schoolrooms:
There it began; and ended
here in his belvedere.

Nothing happened by chance.
He had observed in nature
the phases of the Moon,
and the turning of tides
in celestial patterns
the eye can barely see.
He had travelled in search of worlds,
only to return to the beginning

with a fortune spent on travelling
and another gained in knowledge.
There was a purpose in living:
it was simply to seek itself.

THE FUTURE MAY SEEM WRITTEN

The future may seem written
for the words are clear,
like Arctic sunlight.
And, when whispered,
they become a lover's province.

Swans arch their pride in the water.
Restless spirits seek shelter on stones
worn smooth by mendicants' feet.
Carved in the wood is a prayer.
These things have fallen from favour.

Ivy on the neglected house grows,
like a wilful child.
Someone we knew died there.
At the close of evening
we lose ourselves in thoughts of her.

The cedars are still.
The world now wakes in familiar ways.
Everything is waiting to happen.
Stirring in sleep to the birdsong,
she dreams of music in the park.

Watching her, I speak her names:
Deborah, Debbie, but nothing more.
Her names become her.
One is Knightsbridge velvet,
the other worn lightly in Camden Town.

I see her in her sisters.
Theirs is hers of course.
And others, too, passing by,
may be wished for her,
though there is one moon above.

The clocks in succession strike.
Time may sound precise
but the step on the stair falters.
Sunlight catches glass in its frame:
herself she sees displayed.

The future is written surely in her glance.
Waking eyes are a sparrow's flight
across the know-nothing sky
of new morning.
Her eyes are worlds in motion.

Shades of sunrise surround her
in indigo, azure and purple.
She excels in variations.
The theme is the indelible D,
and light syllables ascending
Toward the woman who knows
more of me than I can see.
The leaf that falls on her
is a change of heart.
Love makes many things happen.

I. TRANSFORMATIONS

Suggestions of Antiquity

SAPPHO'S MOON

The moon within her rose,
slowly drifting westward
until midnight was a fathomless ocean.
And so she was abandoned.
'How easily fooled', she said
of all women in need,
'forgetful of the things that are theirs'.
These things are hers alone,
ever to find the guiding star
leading to the heartland
where none lie alone but by choice.
And then she decides easily
to rise with the sun,
to sleep with the moon.

GENESIS

Before there was a world
there was space.
The universe was possible.
Nothing was certain.

Now the soul may speak
of the change that takes
one life to another.
The gods, who know all
that can be done,
inspire my song
from the Creation
onward to this
that is now.

PYGMALION

See the statue smile.
Touching her,
he feels a tremor in the stone.
And her eyes,
they watch the artist at work.
He speaks to her,
murmuring thoughts
he dare not say aloud,
not to the world he knows.
She is art, and understands
what cannot be spoken.
It is felt too deeply,
like the love he feels for his creation.

BEGGAR'S BOUNTY

(The gods, disguised in rags, experience life on earth)

That shall include the horn-shaped skull
washed on the strand by ocean tides.
And the leaf of the forest,
dried out on the stone ground.
The gawping eyes of toads.
The leap of a hart evading the hunter.
Reflections on clear water,
dazzling Daedalus and son.
Then hearing celestial sounds
in cedar and sycamore.

There are things to lose
in the dream of freedom.

THE BACCHAE

The wind that shook the vines
raised the skirts of women,
scrambling to the summit
of their wilder dreams.
The god of abandon
makes madness of everything.
In this state nobody cares.
The silken shreds cling to the gorse.
Satin shoes discarded sink into mud.

The rains that fall on the city
slow the pursuit of men
in search of reason.
Sleep overtakes them.
Without iron and fire
the King is powerless.
All he has he summons,
prepared alone to face the goat-god.
What he sees destroys him.

THE MADNESS OF AJAX

Possession was a dream
they made of everything:
a woman's honour; her shame,
or Troy itself besieged.

All the men were fools
among their own,
turning valour
to the slightest cause.

Then pity one in knowing
he was a hero
for whom all rage was silence
when he fell blindly.

And beneath his feet
a secret river ran.

ORPHEUS APPEARS

On a desolate plain
comes the heavenly song
from the God-gifted one,
lyre in hand,
wrestling with the wind.
He wanders in search of shade
where none is found
on half-barren ground.

The sound of his song
is sure to move heaven
to raise the cypress
among the wild grass
for the sake of harmony
that stills the air
and lulls the wild heart.

All manner of trees
position themselves hurriedly,
arms outstretched in gestures fixed.
their speech is silenced.
Sadness steals through the forest
till the music wakens the world,
opening the eyes of songbirds.

ACTAEON

'How dare he trespass?'
we asked of Actaeon,
knowing all the while
the laws of chance favoured him
to be the one who saw her.
Revealed, ashamed and vengeful,
or he was acting like one forsaken.
It was all leading to the end.
The hunting instinct stirs
the will unleashed from reason,
hurrying to the chase.
Antlered Actaeon has been found wanting.

ORPHEUS DESCENDING

Centaurs are still in Arcadia,
as still as frost.
Into the fissure of earth
goes this life ephemeral,
deeper than the certainties
of the hermit's dream.
The darkness alone
sees Orpheus go down
to the rumoured margin
of an exceptional scene,
returning to find nothing
has changed, except hope.

POSEIDON: *Of Desire*

On the shore he wanders,
having risen from the water.
His anger is said to shake the earth.
But here he is calmed
by the rhythm of the waves
washing the stones till they shine,
his feet feel the pummelling
of sea and shore.
There is heat in the air now
that the Sun has found him.

His heart is fired by a creature
with the grace of a sea horse
and the eyes of the woman
she becomes, approaching him.
She is of the earth,
and may drown in the deeps
were he to take her down.
When his shadow falls on her
as a lyre bird she flies.
His tears turn tempest of the day.

SYSYPHUS: *Of Punishment*

Slowly the stone begins to roll.
the gathering crows applauds
until scattered by the crash.
The fall was foretold.
We know how it shall end.
The ascent was ever uncertain,
An incline too severe
for mortal hands to raise
the weight of the world.
A god-like task for a man,
that casts its curse in memory.
The stone has no forgiving.

MINERVA: *Of Wisdom*

And the multitudes, where are they?
I am with them in the half-light.
I, the almost invisible,
nameless as one among many.
Where others dare to declare
I am silent, an abandoned orphan
who cannot explain the way I feel,
though my hand may touch the moon
and my tongue has tasted the waters
and my desire is for cities to rise
in the minds of all who imagine
the world is made of dreams.

ANTIGONE: *Of Revenge*

In all her urgency she ventured.
The world beyond the world she knew
was there for the curious kind.
And promises, so loosely bound,
dared to defy expectations
of the cautious claims
that had no right to her mind.
Considering every verity,
she heard what was to be
no more than evasion.

Hers was a truth transforming.
She spoke of restoration,
of changes to be made
in cartographies of the antique.
Moving by implication
into an audacious child,
so unusual in her need
to be undefined,
an available reality, she prayed
in the silence between storms.

Her zest was tempestuous fortune,
and so persuasive the means,
her qualifying mercy
of behaving badly
all for the good of all.

ODYSSEUS: *Of War*

Now is heroic Odysseus
in the battle crowd alone,
approaching fear and awe.
So at a crossroads
is a choice between hazards:
to run is cowardice,
to remain suicide.
Thinking aloud, he says,
'The certainties encircle me;
the wound rests inside my mind.'

ANOTHER HOMERIC MOMENT

Fell the shining spear of Sarpedon
through infinite space unseen,
aimed for Patroclus, moved by fate –
his horse was struck.
Stilled by shock, then rearing,
Pedarus turned away from life.
Untimely end in agony,
the bleeding wound of the world
torn in flesh and spirit,
as stately as a dance.
All energy earthed,
dying to become dust.

THE FOUNDATION OF THE CITY OF WOMEN

The herdsman stumbled on the stone
that was to become his monument
when all that remained of him
was the rumour of children
born to the women encountered
on the open plains wandering.

They gathered in the hollow
for the winter of storms
after exceptional harvesting.
Their faith withstood the want
and built a citadel of stones
with timber from the wilderness.

Fatherless sons were sent there often
until one day they failed to return.
Their anguish was the cry of wolves
or the shadow of ravens.
Measures were taken against the danger,
with the burning flesh of dead men.

2. AT THE GATES OF XANADU

Suggestions of China

ADVICE TO THE IMAGINATION

Do not tell all you know,
nor give names to everything.
Some truths are unknown,
many lives anonymous.
History is written in fragments.
If one word is remembered
you have discovered a new world,
its clime equitable,
its land fecund,
where fauna move freely
and in abundance.
Snow falls on fast-flowing rivers
where fish ride the crest of white waves.
Do not tell of what you find here,
nor chart it for others to follow.
Speak only in general terms
of another world supposed.
Let readers think your tale romance,
unless, as you write, a shadow falls.
Consider the fate of creatures,
punished for being where they may be found.

THE DREAM OF ADMIRAL ZHENG HE

Sailing to the moon,
their compass the stars shining.
What they find is dust.

Consider the Unanswerable Question.
what we see in the sky is a void,
for never can we read a heavenly mind.

Nor dare we delve into the earth
after such an encounter.
Fury tears at our flesh
while leaves of the fall envelope hope.
The wild dogs howl as they come near
to feast on what remains.

All this happens until memory rests
at the end of all affliction,
by the bounty of Providence.
It sees a thing before it is,
and can ask once again
of the forest: 'Where are the trees?'

[Admiral Zheng He certainly reached Africa and possibly the
Americas long before Columbus.]

VOICES

When the caged birds fly
the trees of the garden quiver
invisible in the ruins.
If a wise man listens
the Emperor hears the truth.

Waking before dawn
he sees empires lost
in a game of chance.
Too late to save the spirit,
he fears the sun will rise no more.

In certain seasons
there are no more desires.
A time of absence approaches.
Everyone is leaving the city behind,
opening now to the world's worst.

At first there is silence
as still as frost.
Into the earth goes down
this life ephemeral.

What rumour is heard,
returning to its source,
raw like a wound,
deeper than a dream?
After the dust had settled
we were not mistaken.

A memory of our time
in fire and confusion
Of the world's ending.
Truth was closer to fear.
In their gilded fevers
we knew they were dreaming
of walking on the moon
when horsemen came.

And the waters flowing
through the darkest eye
with ice and iron
housed among shadows,
tasting temptations,
the first of the season.
Then in view the trees
were moving all who remained,
their emotions shaken
by the sight of the fallen
when all we saw was rain.

IN MEMORY OF LI YUI-SE

The eye of heaven opens
when the silk worm moves.
Harmony is found on earth.
Today is the death of the fire dragon,
though his ashes will not cool.

An old man tends the trees
in a distant province.
Warlords are tamed by ripening fruit,
delicate as ivory queens
in a game of *xiangqi.*

The dust remains on the writing desk
where once a volume lay.
The space will never be filled,
for as a soul departs
there is a shadow still

[Li Yui-Se is the Chinese name for Joseph Needham, author of
the monumental *Science and Civilisation in China.*]

A LADY LAMENTED

The room where once she dreamed is open
to the fallen leaves, scurrying
in half-heard words that lie
like dust gathered in shadows.

About here were her footsteps
not yet still on the marble floor,
its pattern a map of unknown places.
her silk sway was the ocean's swell,

Now calm as the carved memorial
where modestly she sleeps
woven at the sound of her name,
even at the rise of the sun.

A TREASURE OF THE WESTERN HAN DYNASTY

From fire and air one world is made,
from eyes and ears another.
A game of sticks and counters,
unearthed from the tombs, intrigues.
No-one knows the rules.
These things are lost over time.

Discovery is a matter of chance.
So much of history is guessing
in the guise of evidence.
The wise go down the well.
What they find is darkness
with echoes of worlds falling.

A DREAM OF XANADU

Creatures so sleek they glide
lightly on air,
stirring the dust
over base ground
those horses never touch.

Encircled by fire,
they are the sun's possession,
A gift from a god to a king,
they ride till noon,
when, like geese, they gather
beneath the trees
by the waterside.
Moving Steadily
to deceive the eye,
they vanish into the haze.

No-one can imagine the world
seen from the stars,
for no-one has found the path
that leads beyond the mountain heights,
nor yet the trail in the wastes
that is surely heavenward.

Of these things there are whispers.
a song of mysteries is said to be lost.
travellers who leave never return.
Rumours are many and
as varied as the flowers

growing in a well-tended garden.
In Xanadu the bamboo palace pleases
all who dream of her.

A DAY'S WORK FAR FROM THE CITY

At dawn the sky is sea.
The grass we barefoot tread
moves also like the sea,
and the sun is a ship with sails
graciously swelling in fortune,
seeking its familiar course with calm.
We wake in the deeps where, drowning,
we rise toward first light.
All embers of evening ashen,
our vermilion dreams vanish.
Dust in the dawn breeze makes mist
of our company leaving for the day.

Working will mock the song
I heard by night of she
who flew with white wings,
plumed in unforgiving innocence
of the walls enclosing the world,
of the wilderness no-one has seen.

REFLECTIONS ON A WINDOW IN LAN'TIEN

The cricket in her cage
speaks sadly of life.
Living through many seasons,
she seeks the springs of paradise.

Once there were forests
where leaves fell gently.
Now there is carved ivory
encompassing her dreams.

Strangely those human eyes
stare with idle minds
amused by their captive
in natural beauty.

The rain runs down the window pane.
in the kingdom of glass
the river has many streams
flowing from ancestral mountains,

Higher than the fireflies,
as distant as the moon.
the luminous river
is an image of heaven.

OF JADE AND IVORY

A child believes the world is there
waiting to be claimed.
Later we come to wonder
where are those islands
we shall never see
if horizon lines are infinite
and the World's a sphere
not quite perfect?

He thinks toward another life
of jade and ivory,
imagining the journey
through a mind of measureless highways
he gives the name of Nature.
A pattern is proposed
to thoughts that follow
the hand that held the world.

To see as he saw
when his hand touched the paper
making exquisite ideas visible,
a map of the world in motion -
observers may sigh at the irony -
they have seen the Moon
reflecting many moods,
all shades of light and darkness.
An anxiety gathering
in the air of the streets.
Through the dark is felt

the stillness, a warning
to the midday crowd
at the town fountain
of a partial eclipse
suddenly becoming whole.

There is fire across the sky.
then there is an absence.
A child knows another world is here,
And how the Earth is affected.
and everything changes
when the finger dances
caught in the time that was
among a murmur of storms.

The illusion of stillness fools no-one
in the living world all that lives has movement.
We ask what compares with the motion
of the stars in heaven?
And then there is the sun.

A WARRIOR RETURNS FROM BATTLE

When I ran down to the water's edge
the days that had disappeared
as the dust of Tartary fell away
in my longed-for returning.
A ghost no more, but a ragged memory
who embraced his wife with love,
again among my children.

The journey had been in endless noon heat,
a slow march through the world,
encountering omens in the words of men
of desolate haunts where nothing rules.
with abandoned stones from a ruin
I crossed a broken bridge
on my way toward sunrise.

From clear streams I slaked my tongue,
taking care to wash away
the blood of my bare bones.
Fruit I tasted carefully,
avoiding the unfamiliar,
so that I might live to see home
and the peace that I would find there.

SECONDS IN CHINA

Dust has settled in the empty room
where mice have found habitation
among the spiders and spectres
of empires lost in a game of chance.
Once – who knows when –
someone left a handprint in the dust,
a way of making history
in measureless time,
for the moment has yet to pass.

And on the window ledge is a flower
that blooms every equinox
of the year's awakening.
were the window to open
the scent would fill the room.
But in the end there is no-one
who comes to hear the silence.
From the window is a view of the winds
raising the waters of the deluge
where once were plains
and the silken cities.

A child asks of people:
'How can they know what they want
until we show them?'
He is thought by many to be wise.
There are those who are not so sure.
all that shall remain of them is bones.

A time of acceptance is approaching.
in certain seasons
there are no more desires.
Old men alone are wakened
by the chatter of monkeys
for whom victory is a game
to be forgotten at sunrise.
Dogs, like merchants, gather
in the square by the statue
of a mounted warrior.
The monument is European,
and may not survive.
A time of absence is approaching.

Rumours are as wild as jasmine
whose petals fall far from the stem.
Storms beat against the window glass,
tapping out a message
sung simply each time:

Every second in China
Something significant happens.

OF CALM FIRST LIGHT, GROWING

Each world contains so much.
The breed of the bird is rare
when we step out of modesty.
A foot falls on a delicate shell
All in nature is there,
taken by the discovery
seen to be a world in flight
when life itself is broken
in an unsuspecting science.

And coming down in rain the tears.
I picture them, watching the grassland
shiver in the first winds of storming.
Were they not where we gather
those trees might seek shelter
simply in the acceptance
of nature roused from routine
with the sensation of grass
on bare feet in the dew of dawn.
Time at times is motionless
of calm first light, growing.

3. THE STRATFORD VARIATIONS

Suggestions of Shakespeare

PROLOGUE

Say what you have seen with words
that we may understand
what moves the world in harmony
with the laws of transformation.
Say what you have seen
of those who are passing by the door
that is open, like a mouth
that sings of many heavens.

A PLANTAGENET WEB

There are many seasons of discontent
with the truth that victory tells
of the murderous lie mistaken.
A king himself may be victim,
and not only the princes.
Many deaths are unexplained.

Innocence is easily devoured,
a mere matter of regret
when the killing is invisible.
In shadow the trap is set,
the delicate craft of capture
a shaft of sunlight shows.

From the intricacy of the real
a history of stratagems.
A design may turn the weaver's mind.
The pattern is to a purpose
not yet revealed to the fly.
When the spider starts to work, beware.

A MIDSUMMER NIGHT'S REVERIE

Infinite as space,
as strange as moonlight
to delight with a dream,
enchantment falls on innocent eyes
that seek their true intent
for the lost harmony of love

The birds that fly in the forest
are abandoned souls searching
the world beyond reason's bounds
when echoing steps approach
the wakening thoughts of love
where the midsummer light rises.

DANCING AT VERONA

In the end is something remembered,
faintly as with candlelight
flickering when a door opens
into infinite possibilities
that death, like love, can offer.
The dance may seem an act of war.
On the balcony she fell
across the bounds of loyalty.
In the confusion they died
as lovers in arms, still young.
Their tomb a place of pilgrimage
where roses lie in simple rows.

A mandolin plays close by,
unseen among the green of the garden.
A statue stares into the sky,
waiting for the gates to close.
At sunset the statues move,
dancing among memorial stones.

SIR JOHN'S MIDNIGHT

A solitary walker in the park
leaves imprints on the settled snow.
The world can follow the way he went
in circles, like ripples in water,
moving to the still centre
where stands a child alone.

The midnight curfew is the cry
as revellers whisper good nights.
A feasting fool seeks love
on a bed of wine-soaked sleep.

In sober mood he thinks of honour
when summoned to arms.
At the battle charge he runs,
ashamed, from the field
to find his way to midnight.

A ROMAN HOLIDAY

There is talk from the city of plague.
Such stories drift through the countryside,
like the soul-stripping decay of flesh.
What the rats will leave death itself devours.

The sheep that graze in the pasture
have yet to hear of Caesar,
and how he fell out of pride
in a cascade of hailstones.
They hit the ground like gunfire,
and left the carcass bleeding.

There is fire in the heavens
and the murmuring of gods.
A ghost walks from its grave.
A poet is torn to pieces
by an angry Roman crowd.
This is not the usual spring.

A god who fails is dust.
Another wears his laurel crown.

MALVOLIO'S EPIPHANY

Say what you will,
this love he feels is a fever
through his maze of vanities
where they lead him to believe:
the journey ends in her.

There is, she is sure,
no music to compare
with the sound of her songbird
flying from the cage.
He of somber plumage,
maunciple no more, but master
of virtue rewarded by love.

She is, he reads, so coy
in her cryptic letters.
He thinks he is favoured
by his desire to serve
the one he calls mistress well.
Lords may be aleaping
but he reaches for the world.

THE QUEEN OF EGYPT

Flamingos may be glimpsed in flight
through the waters of distant lagoons.
They make waves that stir desire
for elegant company at court.
Men are easily persuaded,
my lord, by feathers, jewels and eyes
till they are possessed by their passion.
I am amused to be thought divine
when secretly stained with intimate blood.
And I raise my skirts to shit.
[Men are shocked to hear this.]
Yet still a moth to a candle flies,
eager wings approaching the flame.
Life so fragile soon passes,
and no-one mourns what is gone.
When the wind parts the curtains
the world reveals its curiosity.
Someone looks in to see my life.

THE MISTRESS OF CAWDOR

Her determined hand feels the stones.
Their strength is in the coldness,
or so she has learned from life.
She has sought the life of stones
with walls to defend her ambition.
From the castle keep the view is long,
as wide as the world itself,
or so it may seem at sunrise.

Early she wakes to seize the time.
Someone will die today
within sight of the crown.
Even now the echo is a scream,
clearly heard, like the wind
that stirs the trees to move closer.

AMLETH

Wild geese return at summer's first,
having wintered south by south-east
for their sanity.
                        All is instinct.
Caged birds are said to turn
in the migrating direction.
Nature adheres to mysteries,
like theatre's superstitions.
Reason is surrendered
to revenge for the heart's sake
when a prince envies his king
the crown uneasily worn.
He imagines murder.
                        Blood drowning
dreams of poison or fire.
The gods must be appeased
by secret sacrifice
perhaps in a forest
where no light appears.

What sprite can do the deed?
That is the question worth hearing.
All else is idle musing
on the outrage of fortune
and a traitor's confession
before the axe falls.
I touch the blade to feel my mortality.

VENETIAN WHISPERS

They spoke of mercy,
making eloquent pleas
that I heard as spoken
in good faith, withdrawing
my knife from the merchant's flesh.
My heart was touched as his was not.
Later I learned of mercy's bound
when none was shown me.
Even my daughter was taken.
I am abandoned again,
my life defiled
in the name of another God.
This has to be the death of things.

Snow was falling out of season,
melting in the waking sun.
The limbs of the beggar were cold.
As a heap of rags he was buried
beneath the waste of the citadel.
The sight of stars in a clear sky
became his dreams to die for.
'I gave you an empire,'
He croaked to the worthies.
Coins were thrown in contempt.
Like a ghost the old man vanished,
but not before warning.
All that I have known is no more
than this, my forfeiture,
he croaked to the worthies.

Their justice mocks my name.
Without a name I am unknown.
My head is dashed against the wall.
I am chained with nails
that tear spirit from flesh.
I am the child behind the wire
waiting to be born.

THE STORM

We sail through the straits
towards the undiscovered,
the-might-have-been journey.
A connection appears
to meet an infinity
afterward if not before.
then to pass into the hills,
and from there the mystery

The boat came to rest on the water.
All night we had rowed in steady rhythm
according to the best of our hearts
that we might leave the island
unseen and in the death-like darkness.

At first light we slept in hope
of being so far beyond captivity.
But all that we had done
was to sail the coast in a circle.
This was for sure the sorcerer's spell.
We cursed our fate in his power.

Secret words spoken bound us.
All within the island was his.
He had made a world for fools
to be enchanted for his purpose.
And that was dark in its beauty.

It hurt the spirit to think of it
when we caught sight of other islands.
Heaven raged for days before we parted.
His magic challenged Providence
with unearthly conceit we feared.
There is no love in unnatural things.

THE MOOR OF VENICE

Love has many shades of darkness,
so many ways of spending night.
He knows too well how betrayal begins
in the depth of a soldier's wound.
A fever burns his pride,
his passion changing position.
A word half-heard opens the eye,
but not to see the sun
when reason sleeps in shame.
A sea crossed to a coast
of unexpected contours.
In glim light all is Africa.

THE FOOL'S APOLOGY

The wolves patrol the midnight streets,
keeping silence like a secret
that is the way to survive
the indifference of nature.
There may be a purpose found
when all that can be happens.
Until then there is the forest
where stealth is the watchword.

They see an old man's madness
that summons the spirit of night
as the wolves reach the city limit.
The king and his daughters,
two of whom are treacherous,
are told in many tales
The fool is he who tells it well.

THE POET'S HAND

Snow falling in spring stills the world
that was listening for birdsong.
Flowers, bewildered, fail so see
the life they were promised underground.
For the poor the answer is written
in the tracks of barefoot children
returning home from a day's labour.

The poet's hand warms at the candle
as the light of his art fades.
If you seek his memorial
then read the life in words.
They were spoken in the fields of youth
before he found taverns to his taste.
Words have no season but always.

4. METRO
Suggestions of the City

CITY OF WORDS

These words I have found
in unlikely places
where voices are more or less
the sound of the city,
a sound of mistaken silence
surrendering nothing beyond
the measureless extreme.
No more an echo
of ocean's horizon.
No less than a song
so rarely heard,
the hum of the crowd
of voices not saying a word
that preferred reality.

The view from here is familiar.
We see how far it is
from the urban ideal,
then we may propose
where to begin living again
A city of cypress easily burns.
A house of glass reflects on us all.
Then there are the cedars,
cool in the shade of noon,
shelter for lovers in a storm.
Though the ground may give way,
the fears of fire and flood and plague.
This city has seen them all.

And we wonder who lives here
where the threads of attachment
are woven in complex patterns.
Who calls the strangers' case
in a city of shadows?

Truth may take every room in the house,
only to be homeless again
now a hard hand directs us.
Some may find a private place
in the light of experience,
the engine of imaginings
written in unsupposed styles.
We seek the stranger within.

Beneath the streets sleeps the anger.
Behind the anger is the blade
glistening in the low light.
When money talks there is a sound
out of the measureless depths.

The walls are whispers
from the world of chances
that float like feathers.
Consider the hope of the hanging man.
He dreams of seas in storm.
His words are wounds:
an autumnal afternoon,
anniversary of war.

What rumour is heard,
returning to source:
raw like a wound,

deeper than a dream?
Late leaves fall on stone and steel.

Better voices speak in the rain
washing those elegant walls.
The woman in her café corner,
accustomed to silence,
smiles beneath the sunflowers
painted on a sea blue wall.
Children are amazed by the rainbow
they follow all the way home.

THE HISTORY OF A CITY

The city tremors before the truth:
we imagine elegance in the making.
Elegance is artifice,
though the artifice tremors
because down lies the disordered
before all that is water.
Beneath the stone is water.
and the city is a ruin,
and the beauty is a ruin
in the making.
Beauty is disordered.
The stone beneath will survive.
Truth lies down,
though these stones will survive
because these stones happened.
All that we imagine happened.

BOSTON SQUARE

In light reflected on water
the other side of the square.
This is where the world is found.
In a furnished apartment
an Italian hat rests by the door.
Pale as dust stockings caress the cane chair.
Steve Reich's exacting patterns play.
and I am reading of the future
while she sees how far it is
to the harbour's end.

We are about to eat from the sea.
A fish caught at first light,
landed as we woke.
Then an afternoon autopsy.
Something delicate and dead.

Now, girded in moonlight,
she takes upon her the shimmering
of something appropriate to the hour.
We walk through the square
where another ocean flows
among the ghosts of merchants
who raise their tricorne hats
as stoutly they stand, eternally
alert to the changes of tide.

GHOST WALKS

[1816: Coleridge collapses in Bath a moment's walk from where
Mary Shelley is writing *Frankenstein, or the New Prometheus*]

The stones that made the colonnades,
the crescents and the squares
in air and light, even as
the humbler dwellings darken.
See how Palladian shadows fall
when imagination walks by.

Speaking of reflections:
on midwinter glass
when we are looking,
listening for the words
to sing the last time
she was there, sharing
the glances given,
passing through the summer's
endless time fading
into September moonlight

In the cool of the Salamander:
a shadow from the street light,
and the approaching tread
through the stonework echoing
the sound of .unfamiliar feet.
On hearing again,
they may not be a stranger's
Or there is no-one,

even as the conversation turns
to further reflections.

*

Coleridge missed the mail coach home,
A long journey was saved,
his spirit nursed to health.
His dreams were fevered of course.
A maid would change his sweat-soaked sheets
after a night of visitations.

Below the window elegance strolled,
planning an evening's quadrille.
The poet's thoughts were measureless
to others, at times to him.
Words were written in candlelight
that the day could not tell.

In the city of his fears
there ran dark waters beneath.
Only the damned may drink.
Their cries for mercy sounding
from abandoned places
where no pleas are heard.

*

Prometheus steals the gift of fire,
angering the gods who punish him.
Another secret science reveals
that life itself might be created
in an unnatural Adam.

A spirited mind understands
how all may read
of the man-made man.
Daring to tell the truth,
Mary Shelley writes of a dream
known of old to the wise,
now received by all who live
outside of Eden, in the imperfect world

BERLIN

Today
Echoes along the wall
in this city of bridges
across history with water flowing
from peace to war and back again.
The government elects its people
as the walls erect their stones.

Yesterday
An artist draws a circle of chalk
and Berlin becomes the moon
with dust on which a poet walks
as an innocent to the gallows,
as a book to be forever unread,
as a song without music,
as a thought without words.

Tomorrow
When the beasts have fled their cages,
making for the forest night.
And the sky is void of stars
until the sun's rising
from memory and the eternal record
of how a people find their city
inside the streets that map the world.

A CROWN FOR THE QUEEN OF ELSEWHERE

New York is a railroad station – Paul Elmer More

My dream, as always, was of Elsewhere,
secret kingdom of the city
in my thoughts of Midtown.
We were walking for a reason
that sleep will not reveal.
The city then became strange
where we were walking,
though it was familiar in the nature
of a dream of a city that is not yet.

These things may be imagined.

Paper fell on Lexington,
floating down graciously,
a leaf from a lover's book
someone had scattered.
In the city are many unlikely things
pleased to remain so.
Travellers wait for ever,
like children in the line of fire.

The gilded lyre birds fly
through the midnight lives
in sight of Union Square.
And desire is indifferent.

many dreamers wake alone.
This city may be at war....

I see no diadems in the crown
of she who seeks her kingdom.
Her life lies elsewhere,
from there outcast, she wakes,
naked and fearful
when cast among thorns
a queen without a country
but the city within.

SOUTH KENSINGTON

In Thurloe Square a flower falls.
The fragrance of the tea she takes
is blown with the dust
in the four o'clock lamplight
when an outer door opens.

A finger poised on the cup
is a pen on parchment
about to make its mark,
A marvel not yet seen
as she waits for someone.
Thoughts of mine move me
when I think of her waiting
even now to go somewhere
within unspoken expectations.
She waits for him, I see.

YORK

And walled within the civilized difference
the descant of choristers,
preserved in patterns of stone
so that histories speak
in several tongues,
each thinking the others barbarous.
There are old incantations
of wounds that words never heal.

This is a city of conflicts
made quaint by time alone.
Though something serious is here
with the years inside revealed.
The rumours pass from hand to hand.
The streets of a city are whispers.
Consider the hope of the hanged man,
or a traveller on whom the fragments fall.

ELSEWHERE AT THE CITY'S BOUNDS

The song she sang by the half-open door,
one melody echoing in the public bar,
or where geese gather.
And midsummer snow
falls on hills' horizon.
And the river is swollen
into the island lanes,
as they were warned.
The birds that fly to the forest
are souls ennobled.
They hear her singing
beneath the moon of Araby.

METRO

The travellers are as rain
in perpetual fall
                    when
there seems nothing more to follow
until we find that silence
                              unexpected
in the centre of the storm.

This history is passing
through the flow of the crowd
toward the end of the line
in the face of departure.

The city goes down unseen
in routines of movement
making the people machine.

Within the motion is a thought
that here may be nowhere.

The last train leaves before time.

CODA

SHADOW

Somewhere in the untended garden
you may be found half in hiding,
the ether of essential spirit,
all earth's material filtered
away with time and touch,
leaving behind the thought,
a word and no more
amid the rumouring
in the wildness of hearts
summoned by your art.

In memory of John Fowles

FIREBIRDS

When the trees fell in the storm
there followed a silence
for a brief eternity beyond
the wildness of human minds.
We found no sense in this.
All we could see was fire.
Scorched feathers clouded the scene
when the flames moved like sea waves
to the shores of another land
far from the dream of Parnassus.

The heat that chokes the throat
burns the song before it sings.
No living creature could hear
the passing of the lost.
Every future was fallen
as the firebirds fled.
There was a haze at noon
and the midnight embers glowed.
What remain are mere shadows.
What they leave behind is everything.

In memory of Jonathan Miller and George Steiner

MEMENTO

I take a leaf from the last of the year,
run my finger down the spine,
then search the veins for meaning.
Here is an abstract of events
as they have taken place
from the Beginning.
Hope was born here.
A failure was seen to die.

This time the trees are still
in Lenten-like denial.
A bitter tranquillity
rests on remembrance.
This is childhood in winter,
returning to make
whatever is possible is welcome.
A gathering of birds will scatter
at the sound of lives abandoned.
Were there music heard
it would be of other times,
knowing there is no time now
to say anything more,
Though a final word falls
when no-one has spoken.

The trail you follow is the things itself
unmasked of metaphor, revealed.
The well-worn track of reality
that seeks a meaning imprisoned

in the stone that serves to block the way.
A word made visible when
whispered between the worlds
where may be found both here and now.
The spring on which a mind may stumble
is the beginning, if not life,
then of the water flowing to infinity
we name as nature, unseen but everywhere.

PROVIDENCE

In her floating skirts she fell
with the perfect rhythm of the swing
that had raised her to the clouds
above the beanstalk trees of childhood.

And the snows fell
in the Atlantic winter
when she skated across the ocean
to Africa in the afternoon
of her seventh Epiphany.

She told her dream stories
to the wild swans,
for those family quarrels
were springtide storms.
But in a girl's memory
are many kinds of fall.

Tearfully she would learn how
the blossom does not return
once the tree is shaken,

So she would hear the sound
of the city-bound express.
its some-time-soon promise
flashing past her innocence revealed.

Then there were no more seasons
but of her own making:

the sight of stars in summer light,
the sure signs of promise
that the storms could not break,
that heat could never burn.
If the word within her grew
as the grass in the meadow grew
there was hope of Providence,
the word that became her life.

JOHN BERRYMAN'S RECOVERY

Berryman nay be found dreaming,
the poet conscious of words
sounding from heaven where
I do not want him to die.

Drinking his depression to death,
the old man is a child again
as the drunkard seeking sobriety,
there being so many futures
with all the ways of recovering.
No life is certain in itself:
Berryman is the poet falling,
never reaching the ice-still river
if an angel intervenes,.
raising him up to understand
a certain life and a wilder one
in homage to ancestral music
becoming his Dream Songs.

Imagining his choice
caught between bridge and water,
the poetry, like paper, flew
from the heart of a broken man
to the whole of a life.

Then there was no more.
What was there remains
for us to follow down
into a mind making sense
at last of all the words
that might be and surely are.